SCOOBY-DOO!

A SCIENCE OF CHEMICAL REACTIONS MYSTERY

THE OVERREACTING GHOST

by Megan Cooley Peterson

illustrated by Dario Brizuela

CAPSTONE PRESS
a capstone imprint

Scooby-Doo and the gang made volcanoes in science class.

"Here goes nothing, Scoob," said Shaggy. "Let's see what happens when we pour vinegar and baking soda into our volcano."

"Rubbles!" exclaimed Scooby.

"Like, wow!" Shaggy said. "It's magic!"

"It's not magic," said Daphne. "It's called a chemical reaction."

"Everything in the universe is made of atoms or groups of atoms called molecules," added Velma. "A chemical reaction happens when bonds between atoms or molecules are formed or broken."

"When certain substances are put together, like vinegar and baking soda, they react," Fred said. "They are called reactants. They combine to form new substances, called products. In this reaction, water and carbon dioxide are the products. The carbon dioxide gas makes the volcano bubble."

FACT FILE

When combined, vinegar and baking soda react spontaneously. But most chemical reactions need energy to get started—activation energy. Heat is one example of activation energy.

"Chemical reactions happen all the time," Daphne said. "Without chemical reactions, life on Earth could not exist."

"Look at plants and trees," Velma continued. "Photosynthesis is a kind of chemical reaction."

"Green plants absorb sunlight," explained Fred. "The light energy changes carbon dioxide and water inside the plant into sugar and oxygen."

"The sugar feeds the plant, and the plant releases the oxygen into the air," Daphne added.

"I wonder what chemical reactions we can use to make a hotdog?" asked Shaggy.

"Rum!" said Scooby.

FACT FILE

A campfire is another type of chemical reaction. Fire provides the activation energy. Oxygen and wood are the reactants. They turn into ash and smoke, which, along with carbon dioxide and water vapor, are the products of the reaction.

A boy in class tapped Velma's arm. "Hey, Velma?"

"Hi, Brian," said Velma. "What's up?"

"Would you like to go to the dance with me on Saturday?" Brian asked.

"I'm working on my science project this weekend," answered Velma. "The science fair is only two weeks away. But thank you for asking."

"Lunch is my favorite class of the day," said Shaggy. "All that talk about chemical reactions made me hungry!"

"Actually," Daphne said, "there are chemical reactions going on inside you right now."

"There are?" Shaggy asked through a mouthful of food.

Fred nodded. "Chemical reactions in your digestive system break down your food. Without chemical reactions, you'd starve."

"Rarve?" Scooby exclaimed.

"Enzymes in your stomach and intestines act like catalysts. Catalysts speed up the chemical reactions, which turn food into nutrients for your body," Velma added.

"Zoinks!" exclaimed Shaggy. "Is that a **g-g-g-ghost?"**

"The dance is cursed!" moaned the ghost in an eerie voice. "Stay away, or dance to your doom!" Then the ghost ripped down the dance banner and disappeared down the hall.

"Come on, gang!" shouted Fred. **"Let's follow that phantom!"**

The gang stood up to follow Fred. Just then Shaggy noticed something on the floor and picked it up. "What a goofy looking cup," he said.

"That's not a cup," said Velma. "It's a beaker from the science lab."

"And possibly our first clue," Fred added. "Let's head to the lab, gang."

"Someone, or something, has broken all the lab equipment," Daphne observed.

"Rhost!" shouted Scooby.

Shaggy pointed to a strange silhouette **"It's the ghost!"** he exclaimed. "It must be flunking science class."

"Like, whew," said Shaggy. "It's only Professor Curie."

"What happened, Professor?" Fred asked.

"Someone vandalized my classroom," she answered. "What a mess."

"Scooby found something," said Velma. "It appears to be table salt. How strange."

Shaggy said, "Salt would taste great on a plate of French fries right now!"

"Whoever broke into my class spilled that salt," said Professor Curie. "A few bottles of hydrogen peroxide have also gone missing."

"Let's follow those footprints," Daphne said. "They might be our next clue."

FACT FILE

Sodium and chlorine gas are poisonous. But when they combine, they make ordinary table salt.

"The footprints lead into the home economics room," Fred said. "But whoever was here is long gone."

Shaggy and Scooby sniffed the air. "Mmmm, cake and bread! Don't try to tell me chemical reactions made these too," joked Shaggy.

"Actually, they did!" said Fred. "All sorts of chemical reactions happen when you bake something."

"Yeast and sugar are often used to make bread," Velma said. "They are the reactants. The yeast eats the sugar and releases the products carbon dioxide and ethanol. Carbon dioxide bubbles make the bread rise."

"What time should we head to the dance on Saturday?" asked Velma.

"I thought you were working on your science project," Daphne said.

"Change of plans," answered Velma. "We've got to catch that ghost at the dance."

"A phantom doing the foxtrot?" gulped Shaggy. "I think I'll leave my dancing shoes at home."

"We go where the mystery takes us, Shaggy," said Fred.
"Come on, gang. Let's go buy our tickets."

"Not if the ghoul gets us first!" Shaggy said, pointing.

"Creepers!" exclaimed Daphne. **"Follow that ghost!"**

The gang ran down the hall after the ghost, but they couldn't catch him.

"What happened?" Fred asked.

"The ghost destroyed my ticket table!" explained the gym teacher. "Maybe we should cancel the dance."

Daphne took a closer look at the table. "This table's been completely rusted!"

"That's a spooky trick he played," said Shaggy.

"It's not a trick, just a chemical reaction," Velma said as she typed on her tablet.

"That again?" Shaggy asked.

"Velma's right," Daphne said. "Rust is made when iron reacts with water and oxygen. When iron rusts, the iron atoms give electrons to the oxygen atoms. This transfer of electrons makes iron oxide, also known as rust."

"And look," said Shaggy. "There's more salt on the floor."

"Ralt," agreed Scooby, licking his lips. "Rum!"

"Just as I suspected," Velma said. "It says here that a chemical reaction using hydrogen peroxide and table salt can quickly rust some metals."

"Hey," said Shaggy. "Someone left behind a crossword puzzle. Too bad it's already been solved."

"That's not a crossword puzzle," Daphne said. "It's the periodic table."

"How can a piece of paper also be a table?" Shaggy wondered. "It wouldn't be very sturdy."

Velma shook her head. "The periodic table is a chart that lists 118 known elements. An element is a substance that cannot be broken down into simpler substances. Helium and oxygen are examples of elements."

"Look," said Fred. "There's something written on the back."

"Chapters one and two due on Monday," read Daphne. "It must be a homework assignment."

Fred scratched his head. "First the beaker and now the periodic table. I think Professor Curie knows more than she's letting on."

"Professor Curie's about to go home for the day," said Fred.

"Too bad," Shaggy said. "Guess we'll have to skip this mystery. How about a snack at the diner instead?"

"Not so fast," said Daphne. "What is Professor Curie carrying?"

"It looks like a ghost costume!" exclaimed Velma.

"Come on, gang!" shouted Fred. "We can't let her get away!"

"Professor Curie?" Daphne asked. "Why do you have a ghost costume?"

"It's not mine—it wouldn't fit me," said the professor. "I found it lying outside my classroom door. I think it belongs to whoever destroyed my lab."

"The pieces of this mystery are beginning to react," Velma said.

"And I've got a plan," Fred said. "Professor Curie, would you be willing to help us catch this ghost?"

"Absolutely!" said the professor.

On Saturday night the gang got ready for the dance.

"Yikes!" cried Shaggy. "I spilled pizza sauce on my grooviest shirt. Guess I have to skip the dance."

"Re roo," agreed Scooby.

"You're not getting out of it that easily," Velma said. "I know how we can solve this problem."

"Please don't say chemical reaction," muttered Shaggy.

"We can use a chemical reaction!" exclaimed Velma.

"Velma's right," said Fred. "Chemical reactions between the detergent and water clean your clothes."

"Water has a high surface tension," Daphne explained. "This means that water molecules like to stick together. That's why water forms into droplets."

"Detergent loosens the surface tension of water. It separates the water molecules," Velma continued. "In a way, detergent makes the water wetter! The water molecules can then seep into dirty clothes more easily."

"Enzymes in detergent also break down stuck-on food," added Daphne.

"The dance starts soon, gang," Fred said. "Let's wash Shaggy's shirt and go solve this mystery!"

FACT FILE

Without chemical reactions, there would be no water. A water molecule is made of one oxygen atom and two hydrogen atoms. When these atoms join together, the product they make is water.

23

"Like, what's the plan?" Shaggy asked. "Is there a chemical reaction that can change the ghost into a harmless little bunny?"

Scooby giggled.

"No," said Velma. "But Professor Curie helped us come up with a chemical reaction to trap it! When we combine these substances, they'll make slippery foam."

"And then the ghost will slide right into our net," added Daphne.

"Man, I hope this ghost shows up soon," Shaggy said. "Or I might have to chemically react myself right out of here."

"Let's see who this ghost really is," Fred said. Scooby pulled off the ghost's mask.

"Brian?" Velma cried.

"Look! He was carrying the stolen hydrogen peroxide and salt," observed Daphne. "I bet he used them to rust the ticket table."

"Why'd you do it?" Fred asked.

Brian shrugged. "Velma wouldn't go to the dance with me. So I didn't want anyone else to go, either."

"Brian used chemical reactions to trick everyone into believing he was a ghost," Daphne said.

SALT

"And I would've gotten away with it if it weren't for you meddling classmates!" said Brian.

"I have a question," Shaggy said. "Like, what were you doing in the home economics room?"

Brian shrugged. "Pretending to be a ghost is hard work. I got hungry."

"I can relate," said Shaggy. "Now, can we get something to eat?"

"Yes, Shaggy," Velma said. "We'll whip up a cake at my house."

"Now that is a chemical reaction I could go for!" Shaggy said.

THE END

GLOSSARY

atom (AT-uhm)—the smallest particle of an element

carbon dioxide (KAHR-buhn dy-AHK-syd)—a colorless, odorless gas that people and animals breathe out; plants take in carbon dioxide because they need it to live

catalyst (KAT-uh-list)—a substance that speeds up a chemical reaction without being used up by the chemical reaction

chemical reaction (KE-muh-kuhl ree-AK-shuhn)—a process in which one or more substances are made into a new substance or substances

electron (e-LEK-tron)—a tiny particle in an atom that travels around the nucleus

element (E-luh-muhnt)—a basic substance in chemistry that cannot be split into simpler substances

energy (E-nuhr-jee)—the ability to do work, such as moving things or giving heat or light

enzyme (EN-zime)—a special protein that speeds up chemical reactions (such as digestion) in the body

ethanol (ETH-uh-nal)—a biofuel made from crops such as corn and sugarcane

hydrogen peroxide (HYE-druh-juhn puh-ROCKS-eyed)—a liquid used to kill germs; the chemical formula is H_2O_2

molecule (MOL-uh-kyool)—the atoms making up the smallest unit of a substance; H_2O is a molecule of water

nutrient (NOO-tree-uhnt)—substances, such as vitamins, that plants and animals need for good health

photosynthesis (foh-toh-SIN-thuh-siss)—process by which plants make food using sunlight, carbon dioxide, and water

tension (TEN-shuhn)—the stress on a structure resulting from stretching or pulling

SCIENCE AND ENGINEERING PRACTICES

I. Asking questions (for science) and defining problems (for engineering)

2. Developing and using models

3. Planning and carrying out investigations

4. Analyzing and interpreting data

5. Using mathematics and computational thinking

6. Constructing explanations (for science) and designing solutions (for engineering)

7. Engaging in argument from evidence

8. Obtaining, evaluating, and communicating information

Next Generation Science Standards

READ MORE

Biskup, Agnieszka. *Super Cool Chemical Reaction Activities with Max Axiom.* Max Axiom Science and Engineering Activities. North Mankato, Minn.: Capstone Press, 2015.

Snedden, Robert. *Chemical Engineering and Chain Reactions.* Engineering in Action. St. Catharines, Ontario: Crabtree Publishing, 2014.

Winterberg, Jenna. *Chemical Reactions.* Huntington Beach, Calif.: Teacher Created Materials, 2015.

INTERNET SITES

FactHound offers a safe, fun way to find Internet sites related to this book. All of the sites on FactHound have been researched by our staff.

Here's all you do:

Visit *www.facthound.com*

Type in this code: 9781515736974

Super-cool **stuff!** Check out projects, games and lots more at **www.capstonekids.com**

INDEX

Thanks to our adviser for his expertise, research, and advice:
Paul Ohmann, PhD, Associate Professor of Physics
University of St. Thomas, St. Paul, Minnesota

Published in 2017 by Capstone Press, A Capstone Imprint
1710 Roe Crest Drive, North Mankato, Minnesota 56003
www.mycapstone.com

Library of Congress Cataloging-in-Publication Data
is available on the Library of Congress website.
ISBN: 978-1-5157-3697-4 (library hardcover)
978-1-5157-3701-8 (paperback)
978-1-5157-3713-1 (ebook)
Summary: There's a ghost on the loose at school! Explosions in the science room, metal turning to
rust, cakes burning in the cooking lab … is the ghost to blame? Join the gang as they investigate the
spooky mystery and catch the ghost in the act of causing chemical reactions!

Editorial Credits
Editor: Kristen Mohn
Designer: Ashlee Suker
Creative Director: Nathan Gassman
Production Specialist: Laura Manthe
The illustrations in this book were created digitally.

Printed in the United States of America.
010051S17

OTHER TITLES IN THIS SET:

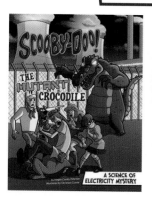

THE MUTANT CROCODILE
A SCIENCE OF ELECTRICITY MYSTERY

SCOOBY-DOO! THE ANGRY ALIEN
A SCIENCE OF LIGHT MYSTERY

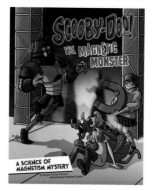

SCOOBY-DOO! THE MAGNETIC MONSTER
A SCIENCE OF MAGNETISM MYSTERY

SCOOBY-DOO! REVENGE FROM A WATERY GRAVE
A STATES OF MATTER MYSTERY